STECK-VAUGHN

Great Challenges

Henry Billings

Melissa Stone

STECK-VAUGHN
C O M P A N Y
A subsidiary of National Education Corporation

Books in this series:

Great Adventures
Great Challenges
Great Firsts
Great Heroes

Acknowledgments

Supervising Editor
Diane Sharpe
Project Editor
Teresa Turner
Designer
Sharon Golden
Photo Editor
Margie Matejcik
Electronic Production
Alan Klemp
Illustration Credits
Gary McElhaney Pp. 2-5; 60-62, 65
Meryl Rosner Pp. 8-9, 11, 13; 32-33, 35, 37
Cover Illustration
Terrell Powell
Photo Credits
Pp. 16, 19 Culver Pictures; pp. 20, 21 UPI/Bettmann Newsphotos; pp. 24, 27 Culver Pictures; p. 29 The Bettmann Archive; pp. 40, 43, 45 UPI/Bettmann Newsphotos; p.48 Thomas J. Abercrombie © The National Geographic Society; p. 49 AP/Wide World; p. 51 UPI/Bettmann Newsphotos; p. 54 © Breese/Gamma Liaison; pp. 55, 57 © Gerry Ellis/Ellis Wildlife Collection; p. 68 UPI/Bettmann Newsphotos; p. 70 © Alon Reininger/DPI; p. 71 © David Turnley/Black Star; p. 74 UPI/Bettmann Newsphotos; p. 76 AP/Wide World; p. 77 UPI/Bettmann Newsphotos; p.80 © Jay Mather/Sygma; p. 81 © Dale Jorgenson/Tom Stack; p. 82 © Jay Mather/Sygma; p.83 AP/Wide World.

ISBN 0-8114-4689-1

Contents

A Voice for Justice

Ida Wells, the owner of a newspaper in Tennessee, was sitting in her office on March 9, 1892. A man came running down the street. He opened the door and rushed to Wells's desk. "Terrible news," he told Ida. "Three men have been **lynched**."

Wells felt a shiver down her back. When a man was accused of a **crime**, he had the right to a **trial**. But sometimes angry **mobs** wouldn't wait for the trial. They would attack and kill the man themselves. That kind of killing was called a lynching.

Looking for the Truth

Most lynch mobs were white, and most of the people who were lynched were African-Americans. Wells knew it was not fair. Still, like most people, she believed people who were lynched were **criminals**. "Do you know the names of the men?" she asked.

"Calvin McDowell, Will Steward, and Tom Moss," the man told her.

Wells **gasped**. These men were not criminals. They were some of the best businessmen in Memphis. They owned the People's Grocery Company. Tom Moss was one of Ida Wells's best friends. His wife was like a sister to her.

"I have to find out what happened," Wells thought. "I have to find out why Tom was killed."

Wells went to city leaders. She asked them about the lynchings. "Black men are lynched when they attack white women," she was told. "That's the only time it happens."

Wells knew this was not true. Tom Moss had never attacked anyone. Neither had Calvin McDowell or Will Steward. They were among the most respected African-American men in Memphis.

No Justice

Wells knew she had to do something to stop lynchings. She decided to use her newspaper, the Memphis Free Speech, to spread the word. Week after week she wrote about lynchings. She printed Tom Moss's last words, "Tell my people to go West – there is no **justice** for them here." Wells told African-Americans to move to Oklahoma **Territory**. Many African-American families did leave Tennessee for Oklahoma.

Wells also told blacks not to buy things from white businesses. She told them not to use city services.

"Stand up and fight for your rights," she said. "If you don't fight, things will never change!"

In May 1892, Wells took a trip to New York City. While she was gone, a mob of white people stormed into the offices of the Memphis Free Speech. They set

fire to the building. They warned Wells not to return to Memphis. "If you come back, we'll lynch you like we lynched Tom Moss," one growled.

Keeping Up The Fight

Wells knew she could not return to Memphis. But she also knew she could not be silent. She had to keep up her fight against lynchings. She kept writing articles about it. These were printed in newspapers across the country. She also began to give speeches. She even took a trip to England to win support for her cause.

In 1895, Wells married Ferdinand Barnett. The couple settled in Chicago and had four children. This didn't keep Wells-Barnett from continuing to speak out. She helped set up the NAACP. She joined the National Equal Rights League and the Afro-American Council. And through it all, she never forgot Tom Moss. She spoke out against lynchings until she died in 1931. Her **courageous** voice helped awaken people to the **horror** of lynchings in America.

Do You Remember?

■ In the blank, write the letter of the best ending for each sentence.

_____ 1. Ida Wells owned a
  a. grocery store.   b. hotel.   c. newspaper.

_____ 2. Most people who were lynched were
  a. Chinese.   b. African-American.   c. white.

_____ 3. Week after week, Ida Wells wrote about
  a. lynchings.   b. hospitals.   c. New York City.

_____ 4. Tom Moss told other African-Americans to go
  a. to New England.   b. West.   c. to Africa.

_____ 5. Some white people burned Wells's
  a. home.   b. school.   c. office.

Express Yourself

■ Ida Wells-Barnett put her life in danger to speak out against lynching. Have you or someone you know ever spoken out against something that wasn't fair? Use the lines below to tell about what happened.

_____

_____

_____

_____

_____

_____

_____

_____

Exploring Words

■ Use the clues to complete the puzzle. Choose from the words in the box.

Word Box
lynched
crime
trial
mobs
gasped
Territory
criminals
justice
courageous
horror

Across

4. an area of land that is part of the United States
5. crowds
6. people who break the law
9. something that causes great fear
10. drew in the breath suddenly

Down

1. what is right and fair
2. something that is against the law
3. brave
7. killed without having his or her day in court
8. the judging of a case in a court of law

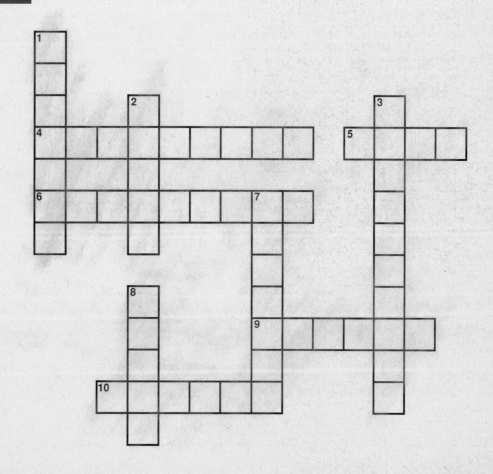

A Teacher for Life

Nine-year-old Anne Sullivan walked into the Tewksbury, Massachusetts **poorhouse**. All around her lay dirty women dressed in rags. Some were sick. Many were **insane**.

"This is your new home," a woman said. "Get used to it."

Anne brushed away a tear. She knew there was no place else for her to go. Her mother was dead, and her father could not take care of her. She had no skills and no money. To make matters worse, she was half blind.

"I may be here now, but I won't be here forever," she told herself. "I'm going to school when I grow up. I'm going to get out of here and do something important with my life."

A New Life

Anne stayed in the Tewksbury poorhouse for four years. She was very unhappy there. The rooms were cold, and the food was often spoiled. Anne **longed** to get out. At last, in 1880, her chance came. Several state leaders came to the poorhouse. Anne threw herself at these men crying, "I want to go to school!" The men got in touch with the Perkins Institution for the Blind in Boston. They arranged for Anne to move to this school.

Anne was thrilled, but she was also frightened. What if she couldn't keep up with the lessons? What if the other children laughed at her? To hide her fear, Anne pretended not to care about anything. She fought with other students. She broke school rules. She talked back to the teachers.

It took Anne a long time to adjust to life at Perkins. But finally she settled down. She learned to use sign language, a way of talking with the hands, and to read books for the blind. In 1882, she had two eye **operations**. At last she could see well enough to read regular books. In 1886, Anne Sullivan finished her work at Perkins. She was 20 years old. She could do many things. She could read, write, and add. But she still had no money. And she had not been trained for a job.

"Perhaps you could study to become a teacher," said Michael Anagnos, the head of the Perkins school.

"I do not want to teach," Anne told him. "I have spent enough time in school. I want to get out into the world."

"Perhaps you could care for other people's children."

"I would rather wash dishes than be a **nursery maid**," said Anne.

Yet a few months later, Anne became both a teacher and a nursery maid. In fact, she was to become the most famous teacher and nursery maid in the country.

It happened because Anagnos received a letter from the Keller family of Tuscumbia, Alabama. Mr. and Mrs. Keller had a six-year-old daughter named Helen. Helen had been sick as a baby, and the **sickness** left her deaf and blind. She didn't know how to talk. Mr. Keller asked if anyone at Perkins would come work with Helen. Anagnos instantly thought of Anne.

"I think you would be the perfect person to help this child," Anagnos told her. "Please think about it."

Anne did think about it. She thought the offer sounded like an adventure. Besides, she felt sorry for the little girl. Anne agreed to take the job.

The First Step

Anne arrived at the Keller's home on March 3, 1887. She saw Helen standing on the front porch. Helen's hair was not combed, and her dress was dirty. Anne didn't mind that. She had seen plenty of dirt in her life. She was just happy that the child looked healthy. She tried to kiss Helen, but Helen pulled away. "She is an untamed little creature," wrote Anne.

Helen was indeed untamed. She lived in a world of her own. It was a world of darkness, a world without sounds. She did whatever she felt like doing. If anyone tried to stop her, she kicked and clawed. Her parents did not know how to control her. They simply let her do as she pleased. She pinched them and hit them and screamed at them. She grabbed food off their plates. She threw her shoes at them.

Anne wrote, "I saw clearly that it was useless to try to teach her language or anything else until she learned to obey me." So Anne set up certain rules. During meals, Helen was not allowed to eat off other people's plates. Anne also made Helen use a spoon. Each meal became a battle. Again and again Helen would throw the spoon on the floor. Each time Anne would put it back in her hand. Often it took hours just to get through breakfast.

Still, Anne did not give in. And slowly Helen began to accept the rules. One day Anne wrote, "my heart is singing this morning. A **miracle** has happened! The wild little creature of two weeks ago has been changed into a gentle child. The great step has been taken. The little **savage** has learned her first lesson in **obedience**." Now Anne had a new problem. She had to teach Helen language. But how? How could she show her that letters formed words, and that words stood for real things?

Breaking Through

Every day Anne spelled words into Helen's hand. She gave her a doll to hold. Then she spelled D-O-L-L into Helen's hand. Soon Helen could form the letters with her own fingers. She could spell D-O-L-L back into Anne's hand. But for Helen, it was just a game. The letters meant nothing.

Then one day Anne took Helen for a walk. They

came to a water pump. Anne filled a cup with water and let the water spill out into Helen's hands. As she did this, she spelled W-A-T-E-R for Helen. "A new light came over Helen's face," said Anne. "She spelled water several times. Then she dropped on the ground and asked for its name. She asked for my name by pointing. I spelled, "Teacher." All the way back to the house she learned the name of every object she touched. In a few hours she knew thirty new words. She had discovered that words were the key to the outside world."

Anne had broken through into Helen's world. Now she could help Helen break out into the larger world around her. For the next 48 years Anne worked with Helen. She taught her to form complete sentences. She **described** everything she saw to Helen. She read books to her. She showed her how to write letters. When Helen was accepted as a student by Radcliffe College in 1900, Anne went with her. During classes she spelled the professors' words into Helen's hands.

By this time, Anne's own eyes were growing bad again. Yet she kept reading to Helen, sometimes for five hours a day. Anne loved Helen more than anyone else in the world. The two had a special tie that nothing could break. When Anne Sullivan died in 1936, the world lost one of the greatest teachers ever.

Do You Remember?

■ Read each sentence below. Write **T** if the sentence is true. Write **F** if the sentence is false.

_____ 1. Anne Sullivan was happy in the Tewksbury poorhouse.

_____ 2. Anne had two eye operations.

_____ 3. Helen Keller was born blind and deaf.

_____ 4. The Kellers lived in Alabama.

_____ 5. Anne let Helen do whatever she felt like doing.

_____ 6. Anne let Helen eat off other people's plates.

_____ 7. Helen went to Radcliffe College.

_____ 8. Anne went to Radcliffe with Helen.

Critical Thinking – Main Ideas

■ Underline the two most important ideas from the story.

1. The poorhouse where Anne Sullivan grew up is in Tewksbury, Massachusetts.

2. Anne Sullivan did not want to be a teacher.

3. Anne Sullivan taught Helen Keller about language and life.

4. The Keller family lived in Alabama.

5. Anne Sullivan was a great teacher.

Exploring Words

■ Choose the correct word from the box to complete each sentence.

operations	insane	miracle	described	sickness
poorhouse	savage	longed	obedience	nursery maid

1. A place where poor people can live and get help is a

   _____.

2. If you wanted something very much, you _____ for it.

3. Doing what you have been told to do is _____.

4. Being sick is _____.

5. A happening that is amazing and wonderful is a _____.

6. A woman who is hired to take care of children is a _____.

7. If someone's mind is not well, that person is _____.

8. Doctors perform _____ to help people who are hurt or sick.

9. If you have told about something, you have _____ it.

10. A person whose way of life is rough and wild is a _____.

Champion of Women's Rights

Mrs. Emmaline Pankhurst could not believe her eyes. The girls in the Manchester, England, poorhouse were wearing thin little dresses with no sleeves.

"It's the middle of winter!" Mrs. Pankhurst cried. "Why are you dressed like this?"

"We have no warm clothes," said one girl. "We have no nightgowns, either."

Mrs. Pankhurst went to the women who cared for the girls. "What is going on?" she **demanded**.

"Well, our money comes from the men who run this place," said one woman. "I could never ask men for things like underwear and nightgowns. It wouldn't be **proper**."

A Bitter Fight

Mrs. Pankhurst shook with anger. "That is the problem with women," she thought. "We are afraid of men. But we shouldn't be! We have been silent too long! It's time we spoke up! It's time we demanded our rights!"

Mrs. Pankhurst decided to take up the fight for women's rights. She believed that women would never really be free until they had the right to **vote**. This right is called **suffrage**. In 1894, women in England did not have suffrage. Mrs. Pankhurst began by gathering small groups of women together. These women demanded the right to vote.

In 1898, Mrs. Pankhurst's husband died. She was left alone with four children. Still, she did not stop fighting. In 1903, she set up the Women's Social and Political Union. It supported lawmakers who favored women's suffrage. Mrs. Pankhurst traveled all over the country to win support for the cause.

In January 1908, she went to the town of Devon. An **election** was being held there. One of the **candidates** favored women's suffrage. Mrs. Pankhurst worked hard to help him win the election. When he did, Mrs. Pankhurst was happy. She stood in the streets, cheering and waving with another woman. Suddenly a gang of angry young men appeared. Their candidate had lost the election. "Those women did it!" they cried. "They're the reason we lost!"

Mrs. Pankhurst tried to run away, but it was too late. The men grabbed her and hit her over the head. They threw her to the ground. Luckily, a police officer came by. He saved Mrs. Pankhurst from the angry crowd. Her **ankle** was badly hurt. Her clothes were torn. And her head ached with pain. Still, she promised to keep fighting. "I'll never give up!" she cried.

Mrs. Pankhurst is arrested.

Going To Prison

One month after the **beating** in Devon, Mrs. Pankhurst went to London. Her ankle was still very sore. She could hardly walk. Still, she dragged herself through the streets. She wanted to visit London lawmakers. But they did not want to see her. Before she arrived at their offices, they had her arrested.

She was taken to a dark, dirty prison. There were no windows. There was no fresh air and very little heat. Mrs. Pankhurst became sick. She was taken to the hospital. Finally, she was set free.

When she was strong enough, Mrs. Pankhurst returned to the cause. By this time she was becoming famous. More and more women were joining the fight for suffrage. Lawmakers were worried. They didn't want to share their power with women. They warned women to stop causing trouble. "If you don't, we will send you all to jail," said one man.

"Go ahead!" cried Mrs. Pankhurst. "It wouldn't matter if you had power to send us to prison, not for six months, but for six years, for sixteen years, or for the whole of our lives. Do not think you could stop this fight."

Mrs. Pankhurst led huge marches through the streets. Again and again she and her followers gathered to demand suffrage. Police tried to hold the women back. They kicked them, hit them, and beat them. They sprayed them with fire hoses. In the next five years, hundreds of women were arrested. But the women did not give up. In fact, they became more determined than ever. They broke into government meetings. They yelled at lawmakers. They broke the windows of those who did not support them.

Striking For Freedom

In 1913, Mrs. Pankhurst was arrested again. She was accused of trying to harm the government. "I have no sense of **guilt**," she said. "I feel I have done my **duty**. I look on myself as a prisoner of war."

The judge sentenced Mrs. Pankhurst to three years in prison. By this time she was 55 years old. Her health was not good. Still, she decided to go on a hunger strike. She refused to eat anything. She did this because she did not want to be in prison. She also did it to draw attention to the cause of women's suffrage.

Mrs. Pankhurst collapses from hunger.

Doctors announced that they would force-feed her. Force-feeding was a cruel and dangerous thing. Doctors put tubes down the women's throats. Then they pumped food into their stomachs. Some women became very ill when they were force-fed. Some suffered damage to their stomachs.

Mrs. Pankhurst was very angry when she heard the doctors' plans. She decided to go on a hunger and water strike. That meant she would not eat or drink. She also went on a sleep strike. She refused to sit down or rest in any way. She just walked around and around her cell. Finally she fainted. Doctors tried to help her, but she pushed them away.

Mrs. Pankhurst speaks to a group in Boston.

Prison leaders let Mrs. Pankhurst return to her home. They waited until she got a little stronger. Then they brought her back to prison. Again she went on strike. So again she was set free for a short while. This happened twelve times in one year.

As time passed, however, English lawmakers began to change their views. They began to understand that women should have the right to vote. At last, in 1928, women were given this right. By this time Mrs. Pankhurst was old and sick. But she was happy. She had helped to win the fight. Because of her and others like her, women in England could now be truly free.

Do You Remember?

■ Read each sentence below. Write **T** if the sentence is true. Write **F** if the sentence is false.

_____ 1. Mrs. Pankhurst stopped fighting for women's rights when her husband died.

_____ 2. Mrs. Pankhurst traveled all over the country to win support for women's suffrage.

_____ 3. A police officer saved Mrs. Pankhurst from an angry crowd in Devon.

_____ 4. Mrs. Pankhurst was never arrested.

_____ 5. Lawmakers wanted to share their power with women.

_____ 6. When Mrs. Pankhurst and her followers marched, the police beat them and sprayed them with fire hoses.

_____ 7. Force-feeding wasn't dangerous.

_____ 8. In 1928, women in England were given the right to vote.

Express Yourself

■ Pretend you are Mrs. Pankhurst. You have been put in jail for demanding the right to vote. Write a letter to a friend explaining why you keep on fighting.

_____

_____

_____

_____

_____

_____

Exploring Words

■ Read each sentence. Fill in the circle next to the best meaning for the word in dark print. If you need help, use the Glossary.

_____ 1. A policeman stopped the **beating**.
    a. hitting   b. meeting   c. singing

_____ 2. Mrs. Pankhurst **demanded** an answer.
    a. made up   b. asked for   c. forgot

_____ 3. The girls at the poorhouse did not have **proper** clothing.
    a. any   b. fancy   c. correct

_____ 4. Mrs. Pankhurst thought women should have the right to **vote**.
    a. hold meetings   b. have jobs   c. help choose leaders

_____ 5. Mrs. Pankhurst led the fight for women's **suffrage** in England.
    a. the right to help choose leaders
    b. the right to have jobs
    c. the right to hold meetings

_____ 6. A man who agreed with Mrs. Pankhurst won the **election**.
    a. game
    b. the choosing of someone for an office
    c. prize

_____ 7. Mrs. Pankhurst worked hard to help the **candidate**.
    a. friend
    b. person who wishes to be named to an office
    c. policeman

_____ 8. Mrs. Pankhurst's **ankle** was hurt.
    a. part of the leg above the foot
    b. part of the arm above the hand
    c. head

_____ 9. Mrs. Pankhurst said that she had no sense of **guilt**.
    a. happiness
    b. being right
    c. feeling of having done something wrong

_____ 10. Mrs. Pankhurst felt it was her **duty** to help women get the vote.
    a. what she should do   b. what she shouldn't do   c. idea

Bottom of the World

R oald Amundsen, a Norwegian explorer, smiled happily to himself. "Soon I will set sail for the North Pole," he thought. "With any luck, I will be the first person ever to reach it!"

Amundsen planned his trip carefully. He mapped out the whole route. He gathered plenty of supplies. But in September 1909, he heard upsetting news. An explorer named Robert Peary had just reached the North Pole.

"There is no point in making the journey now," thought Amundsen sadly. "Peary has beaten me to it." Then he had a new thought. "I know!" he cried. "I'll go to the South Pole instead! No one has been there yet!"

A Head Start

Amundsen did not tell anyone about his change in plans. He knew that another explorer was already planning a trip to the South Pole. This explorer was an Englishman named Robert Scott. Amundsen wanted to beat Scott. By keeping his plans a secret, he hoped to get a head start on Scott.

In the summer of 1910, Amundsen left Norway. Three of his crew knew where they were headed. The other five still thought they were going to the North Pole. When they reached Portugal, Amundsen told them the truth.

"If any of you want to leave, you are free to do so," he said. "I will pay your way back to Norway."

None of the eight men left. They liked the idea of going to the South Pole. They hoped to be the first ones to get there. If they were, it would bring **glory** to themselves and to Norway.

A Bad Decision

When the group reached Australia, Amundsen sent a message to Robert Scott. He told Scott that he was on his way to the South Pole. "This is it," thought Amundsen as he sent the note. "The race is on."

Amundsen and his men continued on to Antarctica. In January 1911, they reached the Ross Ice Shelf. This is a huge field of ice on the edge of Antarctica. It lies 788 miles from the South Pole.

"We will camp here for the winter," Amundsen told his men. "We can't go any further until spring. Scott will have to wait for spring, too. No one can travel when it is this cold."

Indeed, it was **incredibly** cold. The temperature often hit 70 **degrees** below zero. The wind made it seem

Amundsen's ship sails to the Antarctic.

even colder. For six months Amundsen and his men stayed in their camp. At last, in September, the temperature began to rise. On September 7, it seemed almost warm.

"We will leave for the Pole tomorrow," Amundsen announced that day.

"I don't think we should," said Frederick Johansen.

"What do you mean?" asked Amundsen sharply. He did not like anyone to question his **decisions**.

"I don't think winter is over yet," replied Johansen. "In September, Antarctic temperatures often rise for a few days. But spring does not really come until October."

"Nonsense," snapped Amundsen. "We will leave tomorrow."

The men did as Amundsen ordered. On September 8, they set off on dog sleds. Amundsen was thinking about Scott every step of the way. "I wonder if he is in Antarctica yet. I wonder if he is ahead of us."

After three days, the temperature suddenly dropped. It was -56 degrees. The men **struggled** against the cold. The dogs struggled, too. Their breath froze as it left their mouths. Their paws began to bleed. The next day was even colder. It was -67 degrees. The dogs did not have much strength in such weather. The men didn't, either. Amundsen saw that Johansen was right. Winter was not over.

Last Chance

On September 14, the men turned around and headed back to camp. When they got there, most of them were in bad shape. Their hands, feet, noses, and chins were frozen. Kristian Prestrud was in the most pain. His heels were badly frozen. They were covered with big **blisters**. It took days for these blisters to go away and healthy skin to return.

For the next month, Amundsen waited in camp. He wanted to get going. He feared Scott would beat him. Yet he could not **risk** another **false** start. He had to wait until the weather got warmer. At last, on October 20, he couldn't stand it any longer. He had to get moving. The weather that day was pleasant. So Amundsen ordered his men to pack up and head out.

This time the good weather lasted less than two days. Then the temperature dropped to -30. Again the men and dogs suffered. But this time Amundsen did not turn back. This was his last chance. He told his men to keep climbing the mountains of ice that led toward the Pole.

By November 20, the food supply was low. Amundsen picked out the 24 weakest dogs. These dogs were killed and used as food. That left 18 dogs to pull three sleds.

Next a blizzard struck. Day after day the wind and snow blocked out everything. Amundsen ordered the men to keep going. Each step was difficult. There were many hidden cracks in the ice. If the men stepped into one, they might fall to an icy death.

Once one of Amundsen's men thought he saw Scott up ahead. It turned out to be his **imagination**. But the fear of losing the race made Amundsen move faster.

On December 8, they were 100 miles from the South Pole. No one had ever been closer. By December 13, they were only 15 miles away. And on December 14, 1911, they finally reached their **goal**. Amundsen and his men stood at the very bottom of the world. There were no footprints there. There was no English flag. That meant only one thing. They had beaten Scott to the South Pole!

Amundsen and his men stuck the flag of Norway into the snow. They also left a short note for Scott. Then they turned around and headed home. Thirty-five days later Robert Scott arrived at the South Pole. He found the flag and note waiting for him. Robert Scott and his men died on the return journey. Amundsen and his men were luckier. They made it back, and returned to Norway as heroes!

Amundsen and a crew member stand at the South Pole.

Do You Remember?

■ In the blank, write the letter of the best ending for each sentence.

_____ 1. Roald Amundsen was from
        a. England.   b. Australia.   c. Norway.

_____ 2. Amundsen and his men spent the winter
        a. at the North Pole.
        b. on the Ross Ice Shelf.
        c. in Portugal.

_____ 3. Kristian Prestrud had blisters on his
        a. heels.   b. hands.   c. toes.

_____ 4. Amundsen and his men killed 24
        a. birds.   b. seals.   c. dogs.

_____ 5. At the South Pole, Amundsen left
        a. a flag.   b. a sled.   c. an igloo.

Critical Thinking – Fact or Opinion?

■ A **fact** can be proven. An **opinion** is a belief. Opinions cannot be proven. Write **F** before each statement that is a fact. Write **O** before each statement that is an opinion.

_____ 1. It was right of Amundsen to keep his plans a secret.

_____ 2. Amundsen left Norway in the summer of 1910.

_____ 3. Johansen should not have questioned Amundsen's decisions.

_____ 4. Prestrud's heels were badly frozen.

_____ 5. It was wrong of Amundsen to rush his men.

_____ 6. Amundsen and his men ran into a blizzard.

_____ 7. Amundsen worried too much about Scott.

_____ 8. Amundsen and his men reached the South Pole.

Exploring Words

■ Read each sentence. Fill in the circle next to the best meaning for the word in dark print. If you need help, use the Glossary.

_____ 1. Amundsen and his men wanted to bring **glory** to themselves and to Norway.
  a. money   b. great honor   c. blame

_____ 2. The journey to the South Pole was **incredibly** difficult.
  a. only a little
  b. usually
  c. in a way that is hard to believe

_____ 3. It was seventy **degrees** below zero.
  a. measure of temperature
  b. a measure of distance
  c. minutes

_____ 4. Amundsen didn't always make good **decisions**.
  a. fires   b. a kind of food   c. what he decided to do

_____ 5. The men **struggled** in the cold weather.
  a. worked hard   b. laughed   c. fought

_____ 6. Prestrud's **blisters** were painful.
  a. cuts   b. puffed-out pieces of skin   c. broken bones

_____ 7. Amundsen didn't want to **risk** letting Scott get ahead of him.
  a. tell about   b. think about   c. take a chance on

_____ 8. Although the weather got warmer, it was a **false** spring.
  a. late   b. not real   c. pretty

_____ 9. One of Amundsen's men thought he saw Scott, but it was just his **imagination**.
  a. mind making things up   b. friend   c. bad eyes

_____10. Their **goal** was to reach the South Pole.
  a. fear
  b. what they were trying to do
  c. what they were trying not to do

Saving the Children

Doctor Sara Josephine Baker walked through a poor neighborhood in New York City. As she turned the corner, she saw a long line of people coming toward her. They were dressed in black. Most were crying. A few carried flowers. At the head of the line, four men held a small white **coffin**.

Dr. Baker's heart sank when she saw the coffin. "Another life has ended," she thought sadly. "Another baby has died."

A New Idea

Slowly Dr. Baker walked back to her office. She felt terrible. She knew that dozens of babies died in New York City every day. They were born to women in the poorest neighborhoods. When the summer heat hit, these babies didn't stand a chance. The milk in their bottles spoiled. Bugs crawled all over their skin. The babies weren't strong enough to fight off **disease**. One after another, they became sick and died.

In the summer of 1907, the problem was worse than ever. Fifteen hundred babies were dying in New York City each week. As Dr. Baker thought about it, she knew she had to do something. She had to find a way to save the babies.

"Once the babies get sick, it's too late," she thought. "There is usually no way to help them. So I must find a way to keep them from getting sick in the first place."

Dr. Baker believed that most diseases could be **prevented**. She said, "Babies need clean clothes, fresh air, good milk. If they have those things, then most healthy babies will stay healthy."

Dr. Baker worked for the city's health **department**. The department had little extra money to prevent disease. Besides, preventing disease was a strange new idea. In 1908, doctors didn't think about that. They just took care of people who were already sick.

Dr. Baker knew this. So she decided to set up the program herself. She remembered that 30 nurses worked for the city schools. These nurses were free in the summer. Why not use them to teach young mothers about health? Dr. Baker got the city to agree to the idea. In June, 1908, she gathered the nurses together and explained her plan.

"We're going to the Lower East Side," she said.

"There we will visit every family with a new baby."

"What will we tell them?" one nurse asked.

"These families have no way to keep milk from getting sour," Dr. Baker reminded the nurses. "So tell them they don't have to buy milk. Have them try breastfeeding instead. Tell them to give their babies more baths. Most of these families live in old apartment houses. These buildings are very hot, with almost no fresh air. So tell mothers to take their babies for walks every day."

Keeping Babies Healthy

Day after day, Dr. Baker and her nurses walked through hot, dirty streets. They knocked on door after door. At first people were **confused**. Why were nurses visiting healthy babies? Why were they talking about breastfeeding? And why did they think fresh air was so important?

Still, the families tried Dr. Baker's ideas. As the summer went on, they were amazed. Their babies were not dying. They were not even sick! Dr. Baker's plan was working.

By the end of the summer, Dr. Baker's program was a great success. She had saved the lives of 1,200 babies on the Lower East Side. That August, Dr. Baker was asked to be the head of a new government office. It was the first government office ever to deal with child health. As the head of it, Dr. Baker was able to spread her ideas to even more people. In the summer of 1909, she sent nurses all over the city.

In 1911, she took another step. "Breastfeeding is the safest way to feed babies," she said. "But some mothers cannot or will not do it. Those mothers should use good, fresh milk. I want to make sure they do." To do this, Dr. Baker opened 15 milk stations. These stations sold milk at very low prices. In 1911 alone, the milk stations saved the lives of 1,000 babies.

Dying for Love

In 1911, Sara Josephine Baker turned her attention to **foundlings**. These were babies whose parents had died or left them. In 1911, one out of every two foundlings died.

"What is wrong?" Dr. Baker asked herself. "These babies live in hospitals. They are kept clean and warm. They are fed good food. Why are so many of them dying?"

Dr. Baker saw that only one thing was missing from their lives: love. She said, "These babies need **old-fashioned mothering**. They need to be held and **cuddled** and loved." In 1911, this was a bold statement.

At that time, most experts believed that children should not be given much love. These experts thought it would spoil children. Mothers everywhere were being told not to hug or kiss their babies. Dr. Baker knew her words would anger many experts. But she didn't care. She believed she spoke the truth.

In 1912, Dr. Baker set up a **foster** parent program for foundlings. The babies were taken out of the hospital. They were put in homes with loving mothers. Here the children were given plenty of attention. By January of 1913, Dr. Baker announced that this program was a success. One out of two foundlings died in hospitals. But only one in three died in foster homes.

In just five years, Dr. Baker had made a big difference in New York City. In 1913, only one in 12 babies there died before the age of one. This was a lower number than in any other big city in the world. For the next thirty years, Dr. Baker kept working to keep children healthy. When she died in 1945, she had saved the lives of thousands and thousands of babies.

Do You Remember?

■ Read each sentence below. Write **T** if the sentence is true. Write **F** if the sentence is false.

_____ 1. Dr. Baker worked in Chicago, Illinois.

_____ 2. In 1908, most doctors didn't think about preventing disease.

_____ 3. Dr. Baker had nurses visit families with new babies.

_____ 4. Dr. Baker believed babies didn't need fresh air.

_____ 5. Dr. Baker did not believe in breastfeeding.

_____ 6. The milk stations saved the lives of many babies.

_____ 7. Dr. Baker believed that too much love would spoil a baby.

_____ 8. One out of two foundlings died in hospitals.

Express Yourself

■ Pretend that you are the mother or father of a baby. You live in the Lower East Side of New York in 1911. Dr. Baker's ideas have saved your baby's life. Write a letter to Dr. Baker telling how you feel about her.

Dear Dr. Baker,

_____

_____

_____

_____

_____

_____

Exploring Words

■ Use the words in the box to complete the paragraphs. Reread the paragraphs to be sure they make sense.

old-fashioned	foster	disease	prevented	mothering
foundlings	coffins	cuddled	department	confused

Dr. Sara Josephine Baker often saw small white **(1)** _____

being carried through the streets of New York City. This made her very

sad. Dr. Baker began sending nurses to visit poor families. She

(2) _____ the deaths of many babies. She taught mothers how

to keep healthy babies from getting a **(3)** _____ which could kill

them. At first some mothers were **(4)** _____ by Dr. Baker's

ideas. But many mothers listened to her. Their babies stayed well.

In 1908, Dr. Baker left her job at the city health **(5)** _____.

She became head of a new government office. Here Dr. Baker worked

to help **(6)** _____. She took them out of hospitals and put them

in **(7)** _____ homes. She believed that love was an important

part of **(8)** _____ Experts thought that was an

(9) _____ idea. But Dr. Baker proved that babies needed to be

(10) _____.

Queen of the Courts

Althea Gibson walked out of her aunt's apartment in New York City. She saw her Uncle Junie sleeping on the stairs. Bent over him was the leader of a street gang. He was pulling things from Junie's pockets. Twelve-year-old Althea stared at the gang leader. "What are you doing?" she shouted angrily. "That's my uncle! Go bother somebody else if you've got to steal!" Althea ran down the stairs toward her uncle. As she did, the gang leader took a sharpened screwdriver from his pocket. He threw it at Althea. Althea put out her hand to stop it. The screwdriver cut her thumb.

Growing Up Tough

Most people would have been afraid. But Althea was just mad. She helped Junie back into his apartment, then ran down the stairs. She threw herself at the gang leader and began hitting him. He hit back, and soon both of them were covered with blood. The fighting stopped only when neighbors came and broke it up.

This was not the first time Althea Gibson had been in a fight. She lived in a rough part of New York City called Harlem. She was surrounded by thieves and street gangs. She learned at an early age that she had to be tough to stay alive.

Althea hated school. The things she learned there didn't help her on the streets of Harlem. She began cutting classes. No one could make her stop. Her father gave her terrible beatings. But still Althea kept skipping school.

Althea spent most of her time playing basketball and **stickball** with boys from a street gang. Her sister said, "Althea was out in the street all the time. We used to have to drag her back into the house. When other girls were putting on lipstick, she was playing stickball."

Then one day Althea discovered **tennis**. She lived on a play street. In the summer, the police blocked off her street and turned it into a playground. They marked lines for a paddle tennis court. Before long, Althea could beat anyone in the neighborhood.

One day a man named Buddy Walker saw her play. He thought she might be good at regular tennis. So he gave Althea a couple of used tennis rackets. She was good! She hit the ball with great power. Other players stopped their games to watch her play. Less than one year later, she won the New York State Open championship. She was just 14 years old at the time.

Rocky Road

Even in tennis, however, Althea had problems. She played mostly against other black girls. They were not nearly as good as Althea. But Althea was not allowed to play against the best white players. So she fell back into her old ways. She dropped out of school completely. She stayed out late at night. She played cards and shot pool.

Then, in 1946, she got lucky. Two black doctors named Robert Johnson and Hubert Eaton saw her play tennis. They thought she might be the right person to break into all-white tennis.

"There is plenty of **college scholarship** money for young people like you," Dr. Eaton told her.

"That would be great," Althea answered, "except I've never even been to high school."

Dr. Johnson and Dr. Eaton came up with a plan. During the school year, Althea lived with Dr. Eaton. He coached her in tennis. He also made her go to high school. It was hard, but Althea stuck with it. She worked hard at her lessons. When she finished, she was among the top ten in her class.

During the summers, Althea lived with Dr. Johnson. He entered her in as many tennis matches as he could. In 1948, Althea won the **national championship** for black women. She also won a tennis scholarship to Florida A & M **University**.

One day Dr. Eaton said, "Althea, how would you like to play at Forest Hills?"

Forest Hills was just 15 miles from Harlem. But it might as well have been halfway around the world. The people there were very rich. And they were all white. Black people were not allowed to play at Forest Hills. All Althea could say was, "Huh! Who are you kidding?"

"It could happen," said Dr. Eaton. "People are working on it."

"I'm ready any time they are," Althea answered.

Going to the Top

At first, the people at Forest Hills wouldn't let Althea play. But finally they gave in. In 1950, Althea Gibson became the first black player to play at Forest Hills. She lost her second round match to Louise Brough, one of the top players in the world. Althea came within one game of winning the match.

Many people thought Althea had shown great **promise** at Forest Hills. They expected her to become one of the top players in women's tennis right away. But for the next few years, Althea had trouble. Sometimes she was good. Other times she was not so good. In 1953,

Althea receives trophies for winning the National Tennis Games.

she was **ranked** 7th among women tennis players. The next year she dropped to 13th. Then, in 1955, she rose to 8th. Still, she couldn't seem to win a big championship. Althea was ready to quit.

Then she found a new coach. He made some changes in her game. Althea began beating nearly everyone. But could she win a championship?

In 1957, Althea reached the finals of the Wimbledon championship. She was matched against Darlene Hard. The match lasted just 49 minutes. When it ended, Althea was the winner. She raised both arms and said, "At last! At last!"

The United Press reported, "Althea had command of her game right from the start."

Said Hard, "She's the world champion, and she's earned it."

Finally Althea had won a big one. But to her, the biggest game was back at Forest Hills in September. In the 1957 finals there, she again faced Louise Brough. This time, however, Althea came out the winner.

Althea Gibson was now the best woman player in the world. But she had **conquered** more than just the world of tennis. She had conquered the 15 difficult miles between Harlem and Forest Hills.

Do You Remember?

■ In the blank, write the letter of the best ending for each sentence.

_____ 1. Althea grew up in
  a. Mississippi.　　b. England.　　c. New York City.

_____ 2. As a child, Althea Gibson played
  a. polo.　　b. stickball.　　c. squash.

_____ 3. Althea was helped by
  a. two black doctors.
  b. the police.
  c. her grandmother.

_____ 4. Althea was the first black person to
  a. graduate from college.
  b. play at Forest Hills.
  c. become a doctor.

_____ 5. At the 1957 Wimbledon championship, Althea
  a. was not allowed to play.　　b. lost.　　c. won.

Critical Thinking – Finding the Sequence

■ Write **1** before the sentence that tells what happened first in the story. Write **2** before the sentence that tells what happened next, and so on.

_____ Althea won a scholarship to Florida A & M University.

_____ A gang leader threw a sharpened screwdriver at Althea.

_____ Althea won the 1957 Wimbledon championship.

_____ Althea won the New York State Open championship.

_____ Althea beat Louise Brough at Forest Hills.

46

Exploring Words

■ Use the clues to complete the puzzle. Choose from the words in the box.

stickball

tennis

college

scholarship

national

university

promise

ranked

conquered

championship

Across

4. school people go to after high school
5. having to do with a whole nation
6. money given to a student
9. put in order

Down

1. a game played on a court with rackets and a ball
2. got the better of
3. another word for college
4. a contest
7. a game much like baseball
8. signs of becoming very good at something

Jacques Piccard

Exploring Challenger Deep

"**D**o you think we should go ahead with the dive?" Don Walsh asked.

Jacques Piccard thought for a moment. The sea was becoming rough. High waves washed across the deck of the Trieste. **In addition**, some **minor** instruments were broken. But if they stopped now, they would have to put off the dive for months. Jacques Piccard made his choice.

"I'm going to check things out," he said. "If the main **equipment** is in order, we shall dive **immediately**."

Challenger Deep

It was dawn on January 23, 1960. Piccard and Walsh
were aboard the **bathyscaph** Trieste. A bathyscaph is
a special boat that can dive deep under water. The
Trieste had taken some deep dives before. But this
time Piccard planned to take it to the deepest known
place in the world. The spot is called Challenger Deep.
It is seven miles straight down in the Pacific Ocean.
That makes it one mile deeper than the world's highest
mountain is high. As Piccard and Walsh got ready, the
high waves continued. The two men bounced around
inside the bathyscaph. There wasn't much room. Their
cabin measured just three feet across and six feet high.
"Can we really make it?" Piccard wondered. "We have
to be right on target. If we are not, we'll crash into
underwater cliffs before we reach the bottom."

Into the Unknown

At 8:23 A.M. Piccard gave the signal. The dive began. The Trieste sank slowly at first. Then it picked up speed. For a while Piccard could see some light coming through the windows. Then there was darkness. Piccard and Walsh saw tiny plants and animals glowing in the dark. These things gave off their own light, like fireflies in the night.

Piccard and Walsh were all alone. An underwater telephone was their only tie to the main ship. "9:20, **depth** 2,400 feet," reported Piccard. "We have entered a world of **eternal** darkness."

As expected, the temperature inside the Trieste dropped. Piccard and Walsh put on warm clothing. At 4,200 feet, they spotted a leak. Drops of water ran down the wall. Luckily, it soon stopped.

The Trieste kept dropping. It passed the 18,000-foot mark, then the 24,000-foot mark. Walsh glanced at Piccard. "We are at a depth where no one has yet been," he said. Piccard just nodded.

Danger at the Bottom of the Ocean

Piccard turned on the **searchlight**. There was no sign of life anywhere. As the Trieste approached Challenger Deep, Piccard slowed it down. Then, suddenly, Piccard and Walsh heard a dull cracking sound. The cabin began to tremble. The two men looked at each other in fear. Had they hit the bottom too fast and too soon? "Have we touched bottom?" asked Walsh nervously.

"I don't think so. The depth finder hasn't shown anything," answered Piccard.

They waited and listened. They heard nothing else. Then Walsh discovered that a window had cracked.

"In my **opinion**," said Piccard, "it isn't anything serious. Let's go on and we'll see later."

At 12:56 P.M., Piccard said, "Don, look. Here is the bottom."

"Finally," whispered Walsh.

At 1:06 P.M., the Trieste made a perfect landing on the bottom of the ocean. There Piccard and Walsh took some measurements. From a window, they watched a fish swim by. "There is life this far down," thought Piccard in **amazement**. After 20 minutes, the Trieste began its slow climb back to the surface of the ocean. When they arrived, Piccard and Walsh were tired, but happy. They had done what no one else had done. They had viewed the deepest part of the ocean with their own eyes.

Piccard sits inside the Trieste.

Do You Remember?

■ Read each sentence below. Write **T** if the sentence is true. Write **F** if the sentence is false.

_____ 1. There was an underwater telephone on the Trieste.

_____ 2. A window in the Trieste cracked during the dive.

_____ 3. The Trieste crashed into underwater cliffs before it reached the bottom.

_____ 4. Walsh and Piccard found life at the bottom of the ocean.

_____ 5. The Trieste's searchlight broke at the bottom of the ocean.

_____ 6. Walsh and Piccard were the first people ever to reach the bottom of Challenger Deep.

_____ 7. The Trieste stayed at the bottom of Challenger Deep for two days.

_____ 8. Walsh and Piccard died during the slow climb back to the surface of the ocean.

Express Yourself

■ Pretend you are Jacques Piccard. You are about to make the dive to the bottom of the ocean. Write a letter to a friend explaining why you are willing to risk your life to reach Challenger Deep.

Dear _____,

_____

_____

_____

_____

_____

Exploring Words

■ Choose the correct word from the box to complete each sentence.

in addition	eternal	immediately	searchlight	minor
bathyscaph	opinion	amazement	equipment	depth

1. Also means the same thing as _____.

2. Things that have a special use are called _____.

3. If you do something right away, you do it _____.

4. Something that is less important is _____.

5. If something goes on forever, it is _____.

6. We call a measure of how deep something is _____.

7. The feeling of being amazed is _____.

8. A belief is an _____.

9. A special boat that can dive deep under water is a _____.

10. A very bright light is a _____.

Life in
the Wild

Jane Goodall lay in her tent near Kenya's Lake Tanganyika. Her face was covered with **sweat**. Her body shook. Her temperature was 104 degrees. Next to her lay her mother, Vanne Goodall. Like Jane, Vanne had caught **malaria**. Her **fever** was 105 degrees.

"This fever will never end," whispered Vanne weakly.

"But it has to end," said Jane. "I have to get back to work. I have to keep looking for the chimps."

Looking for Answers

Jane Goodall and her mother Vanne had been in Kenya for two months. Jane had come to study wild chimpanzees. African **officials** would not let her live out in the wilderness alone. So Jane's mother had come with her. Jane was only 26 years old. She had never studied wild animals before. Yet she hoped to do what no one else had ever done. She hoped to learn the secrets of how chimpanzees behave.

"There is so much people don't know," Jane thought. "Do chimps live alone or in groups? Do they eat meat? How do they care for their babies? And do they ever get into fights?"

Jane hoped to answer these questions. Every day she walked through the forest looking for chimpanzees. She had to be careful. The thick trees hid many dangers. Leopards and buffalo might attack if they were startled. Jane moved slowly. She tried not to scare any of the animals. Often she heard the "hoos" of nearby chimpanzees. Sometimes she caught sight of a chimpanzee. But it always ran away from her. After two months, Jane was **discouraged**.

"Am I ever going to make any **progress**?" she wondered sadly.

Making Contact

Then came the malaria. Jane and her mother both grew terribly ill. For a few days they feared they would die. At last, however, their fevers broke. Jane returned to the forest in search of the chimps.

This time she got lucky. She found a group of chimps eating **figs** from a fig tree. She expected the chimps to run away in fear. But they didn't. In fact, they came closer and closer. Soon they were only 80 yards away. Jane was very excited, but she forced herself to be quiet. All day she stood still, watching the chimps. That night she raced back to her tent. She told her mother of her discovery. Then she took out some paper. She wrote down everything she had seen.

A Lifetime of Learning

From that day on, Jane made steady progress. Soon she could tell the chimps apart. She gave them each a name to keep track of them. She watched the way these chimps lived. She watched them walk, sleep, and climb. She wanted to learn all she could about them. So she began to try their food. When they ate termites, she ate termites. When they ate ants, she ate ants.

Jane also watched the way chimps treated each other. She saw them play and **groom** each other. She saw mother chimps feeding their babies. And she saw **male** chimps fight each other for control of the group.

After a few months in Kenya, Vanne Goodall decided it was time to go home. She packed her bags and returned to England. Jane hated to see her go. She was lonely without her mother. But she had the chimps to keep her company. And she had her work to keep her busy.

As Jane spent time with the chimps, they slowly lost their fear of her. After eight months, she could come within 50 yards of them. After 14 months, the distance dropped to ten yards. And finally, after 18 months, a chimpanzee walked right into Jane's camp. That was when she knew for sure she had earned the chimps' trust.

For over 20 years Jane Goodall worked in Kenya. She learned many amazing things. She learned that chimps in the wild are very much like people. They eat meat and use tools. They feel many of the same **emotions** that humans do. Jane Goodall's work has shown that humans and chimpanzees are not so different after all.

Do You Remember?

■ In the blank, write the letter of the best ending for each sentence.

_____ 1. Vanne Goodall was Jane's
    a. mother.   b. sister.   c. daughter.

_____ 2. Jane Goodall began studying chimps when she was
    a. 16 years old.   b. 26 years old.   c. 46 years old.

_____ 3. Jane went to Kenya to study chimps in the
    a. zoo.   b. desert.   c. forest.

_____ 4. Jane and her mother were both sick with
    a. malaria.   b. the flu.   c. colds.

_____ 5. Jane learned that chimpanzees are very much like
    a. cats.   b. dogs.   c. people.

Critical Thinking – Drawing Conclusions

■ Finish each sentence by writing the best answer.

1. Jane's mother Vanne came with her to Kenya because _____

_____

2. Jane came to Kenya to study chimpanzees because _____

_____

3. Jane had to be careful in the forest because_____

_____

4. Jane and Vanne Goodall feared they would die because _____

_____

5. Jane tried eating the chimps' food because _____

_____

Exploring Words

■ Use the words in the box to complete the paragraphs. Reread the paragraphs to be sure they make sense.

male	progress	discouraged	fever	sweat
figs	emotions	malaria	officials	groom

Jane Goodall went to Kenya to study chimpanzees. African

(1) _____ let her set up camp near Lake Tanganyika. She

became (2) _____ when she could not get near any chimps.

She felt she was making no (3) _____. Then she came down

with a disease called (4) _____. She had a high

(5) _____. Her face was covered with (6) _____.

Finally Jane began to feel better.

When she was well again, Jane returned to her study of chimps.

Slowly she earned their trust. She saw chimps eating (7) _____

from trees. Later she watched them (8) _____ each other. She

also saw (9) _____ chimps fighting each other. Over time, Jane

learned a great deal about chimps. She discovered that they have many

of the same (10) _____ as people.

Skiing Down Everest

Yuichiro Miura, a Japanese speed skier, raced down the snowy slope at Cervinia, Italy. Faster and faster he skied. He reached a speed of 90 **miles per hour**, then 100, then 107. "I can do it," he thought. "I can win this race. If I do, I'll become the speed-skiing champion of the world." But suddenly Miura lost control. He fell down the steep slope. After tumbling hundreds of yards, he stopped. Somehow he managed to get to his feet again.

"Miura is still alive!" shouted the people watching the race. To them, it seemed like a miracle.

A Great Challenge

Bravely Miura went on with the race. He fell two more times on the way down the mountain. Both times he was going over 105 miles per hour. In the end, he finished sixth. He had lost his chance to be the fastest skiier in the world. Still, Miura was happy. Skiing at Cervinia had given him an idea.

"I need to develop a good **braking system**," he thought. "Then I can push speed skiing to new levels." He decided there was only one safe way to brake at such high speeds. He would use a parachute. No one had ever tried this before, but Miura believed it would work. In 1967, Miura decided to try his plan on Mount Fuji, in Japan. Boldy he climbed up this 12,388-foot mountain. He strapped on his skis. He buckled a parachute onto his back. Then he **hurled** himself down the side of the mountain. It worked! When he opened the parachute, he slowed down. He was able to ski safely down the mountain.

Shortly after that, Miura began looking for new challenges. He wanted to ski down a higher mountain with a steeper slope.

"How about Everest?" asked a friend.

Others laughed when they heard that idea. Mt. Everest is the tallest mountain in the world. It is in Nepal, a country between India and China. It stands 29,028 feet tall. Many people have died just trying to climb it. Surely no one would try to ski down its **deadly** slopes.

But Miura was excited. To him, this sounded like the greatest challenge of all. He decided to give it a try.

The Long, Hard Climb

Miura trained a long time for his trip to Mount Everest. He ran hundreds of miles. He skiied icy trails. He swam in freezing water. He did everything he could to get his body into shape.

In the spring of 1970, he felt ready. He flew to Nepal and began the 100-mile climb to the Mt. Everest Base Camp. With him went 800 workers and several Japanese friends.

Each day the group climbed higher and higher. At high **altitudes**, there is not much **oxygen** in the air. People become weak because of this and sometimes get altitude sickness. Altitude sickness makes people sick to their stomachs, and makes it difficult for them to breathe. One expert told Miura, "Even if you are very tough, once you get past 16,000 feet, you can die of altitude sickness just like that." High altitude can also hurt the heart. In some people, it causes heart attacks. As Miura climbed higher, he thought of all these things. But he refused to be afraid. He remembered his dream. He wanted to become the first person ever to ski down Mt. Everest.

In early April, Miura reached 18,000 feet. He stopped there for two weeks of skiing. He needed to get used to skiing at such high altitudes. While he was there, an accident took place. Some people in the group were caught in an ice slide. Ice on the side of the mountain suddenly gave way. It dropped down into a deep hole. Six of Miura's guides were carried down with it. All six were killed instantly. Everyone in the group was deeply saddened. Some wanted to quit and go home. But Miura kept going. He planned to ski down Mt. Everest or die trying.

Seconds Away From Death

On May 7, 1970, Miura reached an altitude of 26,516 feet. Here, at last, was the South Col. This was a long, steep slope on the south side of the mountain. The slope was 8,000 feet long and covered with hard ice. There were many rocks sticking up out of the ice. This was where Miura planned to start skiing. He hoped to ski down the **entire** length of South Col.

At the bottom of the slope was a huge cliff. If Miura fell over this cliff, he would die. He had to stop before he got there. Miura stood **sideways** on the slope of South Col. He put on his parachute and oxygen mask. Then he leaned over to strap on his skis. The slope was so steep that his shoulder bumped against the icy trail above him.

Miura stared down the mountain for a moment. "In about six seconds my speed should reach between 110 and 125 miles per hour," he thought. "I'll have to open my parachute before that. The edges of my skis can't possibly help me stop on this ice. The parachute is my only chance."

With one quick motion, Miura turned and began skiing down the slope. His skis bounced on the ice.

His legs shook. Still, he managed to stay in control. He pulled the cord on his parachute. It opened. But in the high, thin air, it did not hold him back. Instead, it just dragged along behind him.

Miura tried to brake with his skis. But the edges could not cut into the hard ice. He kept moving straight down the slope, straight for the cliff. In just two minutes, he covered 6,000 feet.

"My braking is hopeless," he thought wildly. "I am moving far too fast."

Then his skis hit something. Down he fell. His back and legs banged against the ice. He slid toward the cliff at a frightening speed. He was just seconds away from **death**. Then, suddenly, he crashed into a large rock. He hit it so hard that he was knocked out.

When Miura awoke, he could hardly believe that he was still alive. But he was! And he was not hurt! He was lying just a few yards from the edge of the cliff. As he lay there, his heart filled with joy. He had done it! He had become the first person ever to ski down Mt. Everest.

Do You Remember?

■ In the blank, write the letter of the best ending for each sentence.

_____ 1. Yuichiro Miura had an idea for a new braking system for speed skiers using
a. weights.   b. parachutes.   c. ski poles.

_____ 2. High altitude can hurt a person's
a. bones.   b. eyes.   c. heart.

_____ 3. While climbing up Mt. Everest, six of Miura's guides
a. died.   b. lost their way.   c. broke their skis.

_____ 4. At the bottom of South Col was a
a. cabin.   b. fence.   c. cliff.

_____ 5. When Miura pulled the cord on his parachute, it
a. did not open.
b. opened, but did not hold him back.
c. opened and brought him safely to a stop.

Express Yourself

■ Pretend you are Yuichiro Miura. You are planning to ski down Mount Everest. Some of your friends think it is a dangerous and foolish idea. Write a letter to one of these friends explaining why you want to ski down Everest.

Dear _____,

_____

_____

_____

_____

_____

Exploring Words

■ Use the clues to complete the puzzle. Choose from the words in the box

miles per hour

braking

system

hurled

deadly

altitudes

oxygen

entire

sideways

death

Across

3. a way of measuring speed
7. the end of life
8. whole
9. able to kill
10. one of the gases in air

Down

1. threw
2. stopping
4. with the side in front
5. high places
6. a group of parts that work together

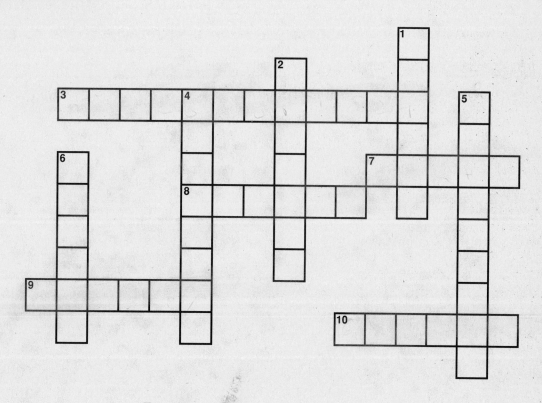

A Call
for
Change

Desmond Tutu walked past a school in Klerksdorp, South Africa. Tutu had never been inside this school. He was black, and the school was open only to whites. Tutu did see several blacks standing outside the building. But they were not waiting to go to class. They were digging through the garbage cans. They were hoping that the white children had thrown out some **scraps** of food.

Tutu was not surprised. He often saw scenes like this. In South Africa, whites got everything. Blacks got only what whites didn't want.

Apartheid keeps black people apart from white people in South Africa.

A Terrible System

As Desmond Tutu grew older, he saw just how bad things were in South Africa. Five out of every six people were black. Yet whites had all the power. Blacks couldn't vote or run for office. They couldn't get good jobs. They couldn't live or play with white people. This system of keeping black people away from white people is called **apartheid**.

Tutu hated apartheid. But he did not hate whites. He knew that some whites were good people. For example, Trevor Huddleston was a good man. Huddleston was an Anglican **priest**. Although he was white, he worked closely with the poor black people in South Africa. During the 1950's, he was the strongest white voice against apartheid.

Over time, Huddleston and Tutu became good friends. In 1957, Tutu decided to quit his job as a teacher. He followed Huddleston's example and became an Anglican priest. Tutu rose rapidly in the Anglican church. In 1976, he became the first black head of an Anglican church. With the job came a fancy house in an all-white neighborhood in Johannesburg. Tutu refused to live in the house. Instead, he moved into a poor black neighborhood called Soweto.

Speaking Out

In 1977, Tutu became a **bishop**. By this time he was speaking out loudly against the South African system. "Anything would be better than apartheid," he said. "It is an **immoral** and **evil** system."

Bishop Tutu hoped change could come peacefully. But he knew this would be hard. He asked for help from other countries. He asked the whole world to take a stand against apartheid. "Do not spend money in South Africa," he cried. "Do not support a government that treats its people so badly."

By the 1980's, many white South Africans hated Tutu. Some made angry phone calls to him. Others said they would kill him. Government leaders made public statements against him. They tried to keep him from traveling outside South Africa. Once they even sent him to jail. Despite all of this, Tutu continued to speak out. Every day he put his life in danger in order to fight for what he believed in.

On The Side Of Justice

In 1984, Bishop Tutu and his followers got a big **boost**. Bishop Tutu was given the Nobel Peace Prize. This **award** honored him for his **courage** and for fighting against apartheid peacefully. Said Bishop Tutu happily, "We are winning! Justice is going to win. We mustn't give up."

Bishop Tutu's award gave new hope to blacks in South Africa. They planned new marches and **strikes**. Soon trouble broke out. Hundreds of people were killed or sent to jail. But the blacks did not give up. They listened to the words of Bishop Tutu and other black leaders. They knew justice was on their side.

Finally, in 1990, the South African government began to change. It began to think about ending apartheid. Bishop Tutu was thrilled. He knew the fight was not over. But progress was being made. At last Bishop Tutu could say, "The walls of apartheid are falling!"

Bishop Tutu stands among girls from his congregation.

Do You Remember?

■ Read each sentence below. Write **T** if the sentence is true. Write **F** if the sentence is false.

_____ 1. Desmond Tutu grew up in South Africa.

_____ 2. Most people in South Africa were white.

_____ 3. Blacks in South Africa could not vote.

_____ 4. Trevor Huddleston was a black Anglican priest.

_____ 5. In 1957, Tutu decided to quit his job as a truck driver.

_____ 6. Tutu refused to live in a rich white neighborhood.

_____ 7. Tutu became a bishop in the Anglican church.

_____ 8. In 1984, Tutu refused to accept the Nobel Peace Prize.

Critical Thinking – Cause and Effect

■ Complete the following sentences.

1. Desmond Tutu had never been inside the school in Klerksdorp because

_____

2. Blacks dug through the garbage cans outside the school in Klerksdorp

because _____

3. Tutu asked other countries to stop spending money in South Africa

because _____

4. Government leaders sent Bishop Tutu to jail because _____

_____

5. Bishop Tutu was given the Nobel Peace Prize because _____

_____

Exploring Words

■ Read each sentence. Fill in the circle next to the best meaning for the word in dark print. If you need help, use the Glossary.

1. They searched for **scraps** of food.
   ○ a. small pieces   ○ b. plates   ○ c. large pieces

2. Desmond Tutu fought against **apartheid**.
   ○ a. keeping black people away from white people
   ○ b. Anglican beliefs
   ○ c. killing animals

3. Trevor Huddleston was a white **priest**.
   ○ a. store owner   ○ b. policeman   ○ c. person of the church

4. Desmond Tutu became a **bishop**.
   ○ a. person in jail.
   ○ b. winner of a prize
   ○ c. important church leader

5. Tutu believed the laws of South Africa were **immoral**.
   ○ a. fair   ○ b. not right   ○ c. wise

6. Tutu said that these laws were **evil**.
   ○ a. very good   ○ b. very bad   ○ c. not important

7. Tutu won a special **award**.
   ○ a. prize   ○ b. car   ○ c. contest

8. The announcement of Tutu's award gave his followers a **boost**.
   ○ a. lift in spirits   ○ b. scare   ○ c. meeting place

9. It took **courage** for Tutu to speak out.
   ○ a. hard work   ○ b. being brave   ○ c. a quick mind

10. The people organized **strikes**.
    ○ a. stopping of work   ○ b. parties   ○ c. games

Perfect Pitch

The doctor looked at five-year-old Jim Abbott. Jim had been born without a right hand. His arm ended at the wrist.

"I'm going to make a special **device** for you," the doctor said to Jim. "It will go on the end of your arm. It will have a metal hook. You can learn to use the hook the way other people use fingers."

"Will I be able to play baseball with it?" Jim asked the doctor.

The doctor smiled. But secretly he felt like crying. He saw no way that a one-handed boy could play baseball.

A Great Challenge

Jim wore the hook for a year and a half. But he hated it. Finally his parents put the hook away. They let Jim learn to do things his way.

"I'm going to be a baseball player," Jim told his parents. "I'm going to be a pitcher." Jim didn't think about his missing hand. He just thought about teaching himself to play baseball.

Jim had a strong left arm. So he could throw a ball well. But catching it was different. He couldn't wear a glove the way other kids did. He wore his glove on his right wrist. After pitching the ball, he slipped his left hand into the glove to catch the ball. To throw a runner out, he rested the ball and glove on his right arm. Then he grabbed the ball from the glove with his left hand and made the throw.

Jim practiced by playing catch with himself. Again and again he threw a baseball against a brick wall. When it bounced back, he slipped on his glove and caught it. As he got better, he moved closer to the wall. In time, Jim learned how to **field** with just one hand.

Making the Big Leagues

Jim turned out to be a great pitcher. He was a star on his high school team in Flint, Michigan. He was an All-American in college. And he helped the United States Olympic baseball team win a gold medal in 1988.

That year, Jim was signed by the California Angels. Most people thought he would stay with the Angels' **minor league** team. Everyone knew Jim had **talent**. But they still didn't think a one-handed pitcher could make it to the big leagues.

During 1989 spring training, Jim pitched well. He even struck out Jose Canseco, a great home run hitter. In March, the Angels announced that Jim Abbott was joining

their **major league** team. He would be one of their starting pitchers.

Some people couldn't believe it. They thought it was just a way to sell tickets.

Jim just said, "I hope to prove them wrong."

Beating the Best

Jim had a slow start with the Angels. He won two games but lost three. Then, on May 17th, he faced his biggest test. The Angels played the Boston Red Sox.

Roger Clemens was pitching for the Sox. Clemens had twice been named the best pitcher in the American League. He had held the major league record for striking out batters. What chance did a **rookie** pitcher like Jim Abbott have against the great Roger Clemens? Jim was nervous about the game. But he wasn't scared. He just went out and threw the best pitches he could. Time after time, he got the batters out.

Meanwhile, Clemens had a rough game. He gave up five runs in the first **inning**. In the third inning, a **relief pitcher** took Clemens's place. But Jim was still pitching beautifully. He pitched a complete game without giving up any runs. He also fielded the ball perfectly.

After that, there were no more doubts about Jim Abbott. By July, people were calling him the best rookie starter in baseball. They stopped thinking about his missing hand. They finally saw that his talent was more important than his **disability**.

Do You Remember?

■ In the blank, write the letter of the best ending for each sentence.

_____ 1. Jim Abbott was born without a
   a. right hand.   b. left arm.   c. right foot.

_____ 2. As a small child, Jim wanted to be a
   a. doctor.   b. baseball player.   c. swimmer.

_____ 3. Jim Abbott helped the 1988 U.S. Olympic baseball team win a
   a. gold medal.   b. silver medal.   c. bronze medal.

_____ 4. In 1988, Jim was signed by the
   a. Boston Red Sox.   b. Texas Rangers.   c. California
                                                        Angels.

_____ 5. Roger Clemens is
   a. a great home run hitter.
   b. Jim's best friend.
   c. a pitcher for the Red Sox.

Express Yourself

■ Pretend you are Jim Abbott. You have been asked to give a speech to children with disabilities. What would you say to them?

_____

_____

_____

_____

_____

_____

Exploring Words

■ Choose the correct word from the box to complete each sentence.

device	minor league	talent	major league	field
rookie	relief pitcher	innings	Meanwhile	disability

1. A _____ takes over for a starting pitcher.

2. If you are able to do something well, you have _____.

3. When you catch or throw a baseball that has been hit by a batter, you

   _____ the ball.

4. A _____ is the most important group of sports teams that

   play each other.

5. A small, simple machine is a _____.

6. Having only one hand is a _____.

7. Baseball games are divided into nine _____.

8. A _____ is a person playing his or her first season in the

   major leagues.

9. _____ means during the same time.

10. A _____ is a group of sports teams usually used by major

    league teams to train players.

Another Way to the Top

The sweat rolled down Mark Wellman's cheeks. The **veins** in his neck stood out. "Eight ... nine ... ten," he groaned to himself.

Wellman set the weights down. He didn't mind all the work and pain. It was worth it to make his arms and shoulders stronger. He wanted to climb El Capitan in California's Yosemite Valley. El Capitan is a wall of rock 3,569 feet high. Few people had ever climbed it. And no one had ever climbed it without the use of his legs.

El Capitan

Wanting to Climb Again

Mark Wellman lost the use of his legs in 1982. He slipped while rock climbing and fell fifty feet. The fall left him **paralyzed** from the waist down. He didn't want to quit rock climbing. But how could a person without the use of his legs climb mountains?

Then one day Wellman picked up a magazine for people who have disabilities. The cover showed a man going up a mountain in a **wheelchair**. Wellman showed the picture to a friend named Mike Corbett. Corbett also loved to climb rocks.

"Would you do something like that?" Corbett asked.

"Yeah," Wellman answered, "But not in a wheelchair."

"Well," said Corbett, "let's figure out a way to get you back on the rock."

Finding a Way

For several days the two men worked on the problem. Like other rock climbers, they would have to be hooked together by ropes. Corbett would lead the way. He would drive metal spikes, called **pitons**, into the rock. The pitons would hold the ropes in place. This is the way all rock climbers climb.

The trick was finding a way for Wellman to pull himself up the wall of rock. He decided to use an eight-inch pull-up bar. The bar could be moved up the rope and locked into place. Wellman would do pull-ups on the bar. After each pull-up, he would move the bar a little higher up the rope. In that way, he could pull himself up the cliff six inches at a time.

Wellman knew he needed **tremendous** strength to make the climb. For six months he lifted weights and swam. He and Corbett also made 35 practice climbs. Finally, they felt ready to take on El Capitan.

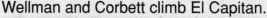

Wellman and Corbett climb El Capitan.

Corbett carries Wellman
on his back.

The Big Climb

They began their climb on July 19, 1989. Slowly they moved up the rock face. Corbett went first. He drove in the pitons. He also carried 200 pounds of tools, food, and sleeping bags. Wellman came next. He pulled himself up a few inches at a time. At the end of each day, both men were **exhausted**. They had to force themselves to eat. They slept hanging from the rock wall.

As they climbed higher, the winds became very strong. At 2,000 feet, they came to a 40-foot **ledge** of rock that stuck out from the wall. There was no way around it. It had to be climbed.

Corbett climbed it first. Then he grabbed the rope and swung Wellman out. As Wellman **dangled** there, he felt his arms and shoulders **straining**. But slowly, using his pull-up bar, he inched his way to the top of the ledge.

After seven days the two men neared the top. When they were just 300 feet away, they ran into trouble. The pitons wouldn't hold in the soft rock. Neither man wanted to quit. So Corbett lifted Wellman onto his back. He had to be careful. If he made one wrong step, they would both tumble into the valley below. But Corbett didn't slip. The two men reached the top safely!

Mark Wellman later said, "I don't **consider** myself disabled. My whole thing in life is finding another way."

Do You Remember?

∎ Read each sentence below. Write **T** if the sentence is true. Write **F** if the sentence is false.

_____ 1. El Capitan is a wall of rock in California's Yosemite Valley.

_____ 2. Mark Wellman lost the use of his legs in a car accident.

_____ 3. Mike Corbett did not like rock climbing.

_____ 4. Mark Wellman trained for six months before making the climb up El Capitan.

_____ 5. During the climb, Corbett carried 200 pounds of supplies.

_____ 6. Near the top of the mountain, Corbett slipped and fell.

_____ 7. It took Wellman and Corbett 20 days to climb El Capitan.

_____ 8. Corbett carried Wellman up the last 300 feet of El Capitan.

Critical Thinking – Finding the Sequence

∎ Write **1** before the sentence that tells what happened first in the story. Write **2** before the sentence that tells what happened next, and so on.

_____ Mark Wellman saw a picture of a man in a wheelchair climbing a mountain.

_____ Mark Wellman slipped while rock climbing and fell.

_____ Mike Corbett drove pitons into the side of El Capitan.

_____ Mike Corbett lifted Mark Wellman onto his back.

_____ Mark Wellman and Mike Corbett made 35 practice climbs.

Exploring Words

■ Use the clues to complete the puzzle. Choose from the words in the box.

veins

paralyzed

wheelchair

pitons

tremendous

exhausted

ledge

dangled

straining

consider

Across

3. very tired
5. a part of a mountain shaped like a shelf
8. these carry blood through your body
9. working as hard as possible
10. metal spikes

Down

1. A chair with wheels used by people who cannot walk
2. hung and swung loosely
4. very great
6. think of
7. not able to move

Glossary

altitudes, page 63
High places are sometimes called altitudes.

amazement, page 51
Amazement is the feeling of being amazed.

ankle, page 18
Your ankle is the part of your leg right above your foot.

apartheid, page 70
Apartheid is a set of rules in South Africa that keeps black people apart from white people.

award, page 71
An award is something given to someone to honor that person for something she or he has done.

bathyscaph, page 49
A bathyscaph is a special boat that can dive deep under water.

beating, page 19
If someone has attacked and hit you, you have had a beating.

bishop, page 70
A bishop is an important leader in some churches.

blisters, page 28
A blister is a puffing out of the skin.

boost, page 71
A boost is something that lifts your spirits and makes you feel better.

braking, page 62
If you are braking, you are trying to stop.

candidates, page 18
A candidate is a person who wishes to be named to an office, such as mayor or president.

championship, page 44
A championship is a contest held to find out who is best at something.

coffin, page 33
A coffin is a box in which a dead person is buried.

college, page 43
A college is a school people go to after high school.

confused, page 35
If you are confused, you feel mixed up and are not sure of things.

conquered, page 45
To have conquered means to have won or to have gotten the better of something.

consider, page 83
To consider means to think of. If you think of someone as your friend, you consider that person your friend.

courage, page 71
Courage is the act of being brave.

courageous, page 5
Courageous means brave.

crime, page 2
A crime is something that is against the law.

criminals, page 3
Criminals are people who do things that are against the law.

cuddled, page 36
To cuddle is to hug or hold close.

dangled, page 83
To dangle means to hang and swing loosely.

deadly, page 63
Something that is deadly is able to kill.

death, page 65
Death is the end of life.

decisions, page 27
Your decisions are the things you have decided to do.

degrees, page 26
A degree is a measure of temperature.

demanded, page 17
If you demanded something, you asked for it as though it were your right.

department, page 34
A department is a part of a government or business.

depth, page 50
Depth is a measure of how deep something is.

described, page 13
To describe something is to tell about it.

device, page 75
A device is a small, simple machine.

disability, page 77
A disability is something that keeps you from doing certain things.

discouraged, page 56
If you feel discouraged, you have lost hope.

disease, page 34
To have a disease is to be sick.

duty, page 20
Duty is what you should do because it is right.

election, page 18
An election is the choosing of someone for an office or honor.

emotions, page 57
Emotions are feelings such as joy and sadness.

entire, page 64
Entire means whole.

equipment, page 48
Equipment means things that have a special use.

eternal, page 50
Eternal means going on forever.

evil, page 70
Evil means very bad.

exhausted, page 83
Exhausted means very tired.

false, page 28
False means not real or true.

fever, page 54
If you have a fever, the temperature of your body is high.

field, page 76
To field means to catch or throw a baseball that has been hit by a batter.

figs, page 56
Figs are a kind of small, sweet fruit.

foster, page 37
Foster parents bring up a child who is not theirs.

foundlings, page 36
Foundlings are babies whose parents have left them.

gasped, page 3
If you gasped, you drew in your breath suddenly.

glory, page 26
Glory is great honor.

goal, page 29
Your goal is what you are trying to do.

groom, page 57
To groom means to make neat and clean.

guilt, page 20
When you have done something wrong, you feel guilt.

horror, page 5
Something that is a horror causes great fear.

hurled, page 62
If you hurled something, you threw it very hard.

imagination, page 29
When you make things up, you use your imagination.

immediately, page 48
Immediately means right away or at once.

immoral, page 70
Immoral means not right.

in addition, page 48
In addition means also.

incredibly, page 26
Incredibly means in a way that is hard to believe. If it was incredibly cold, it was so cold that it was hard to believe.

inning, page 77
An inning is one of the nine parts into which a baseball game is divided.

insane, page 9
Someone whose mind is not well is insane.

justice, page 4
Justice is what is right and fair.

ledge, page 83
A ledge is a part of a mountain shaped like a shelf.

longed, page 10
If you longed for something, you wanted it very much.

lynched, page 2
To lynch means to kill a person without giving that person her or his day in court.

major league, page 77
A major league is the most important group of sports teams that play each other.

malaria, page 54
Malaria is a sickness.

male, page 57
A male is a man or a boy.

meanwhile, page 77
Meanwhile means during the same time.

miles per hour, page 61
Miles per hour means miles for each hour. Speed is measured in miles per hour.

minor, page 48
Minor means less important.

minor league, page 76
A minor league is a group pf sports teams usually used by major league teams to train players.

miracle, page 12
A miracle is a happening that is amazing and wonderful.

mobs, page 2
A mob is a crowd.

mothering, page 36
Mothering means taking care of someone as though you were that person's mother.

national, page 44
National means having to do with a whole nation or country.

nursery maid, page 10
A nursery maid is a woman who is hired to take care of children.

obedience, page 12
Obedience is doing what you have been told to do.

officials, page 55
Officials are people who hold offices.

old-fashioned, page 36
Old-fashioned means out-of-date.

operations, page 10
An operation is something done by doctors to treat a person who is hurt or sick.

opinion, page 51
An opinion is a belief.

oxygen, page 63
Oxygen is one of the gases in air that people need to breathe.

paralyzed, page 81
Paralyzed means not able to move.

pitons, page 82
Pitons are metal spikes used by mountain climbers.

poorhouse, page 9

A poorhouse is a place paid for by the government where poor people can live and get help.

prevented, page 34

If you prevented something, you kept it from happening.

priest, page 70

A priest is a person of the church.

progress, page 56

If you have made progress, you have gotten closer to your goal.

promise, page 44

If you show promise at something, you show signs of becoming very good at it.

proper, page 17

Proper means fitting or polite.

ranked, page 45

If you ranked things, you put them in order. To say that Althea Gibson was ranked seventh among women tennis players means that she was the seventh best player.

relief pitcher, page 77

A relief pitcher is a person who takes over for the starting pitcher when the starting pitcher is tired or not doing well.

risk, page 28

If you risk something, you take a chance on it.

rookie, page 77

A rookie is a person playing his or her first season in the major leagues.

savage, page 12

A savage is a person whose way of life is rough and wild.

scholarship, page 43

A scholarship is money given to a student to help her or him go to college.

scraps, page 69

Scraps are little pieces left over from a whole.

searchlight, page 50

A searchlight is a very bright light.

sickness, page 11

Sickness means being sick.

sideways, page 64

Sideways means with the side in front.

stickball, page 42

Stickball is a game much like baseball.

straining, page 83

Straining means working as hard as possible.

strikes, page 71

A strike is when people stop working to call attention to a problem.

struggled, page 28

If you struggled, you worked very hard.

suffrage, page 18

Suffrage is the right to help choose government leaders.

sweat, page 54

Sweat is water given off through the skin.

system, page 62

A system is a group of parts that work together to do something.

talent, page 76

Talent means being able to do something well.

tennis, page 42

Tennis is a game played on a court with rackets and a ball.

Territory, page 4

A territory is an area of land that is part of the United States, but is not a state.

tremendous, page 82

Tremendous means very great.

trial, page 2

A trial is the judging of a case in a court of law.

university, page 44

A university is a school people go to after high school.

veins, page 80

Your veins carry blood through your body.

vote, page 18

If you have the right to vote, you can help choose the leaders in your government.

wheelchair, page 81

A wheelchair is a chair with wheels used by people who cannot walk.

Chart Your Progress

Stories	Do You Remember?	Exploring Words	Critical Thinking	Express Yourself	Score
A Voice for Justice					/20
A Teacher for Life					/20
Champion of Women's Rights					/23
Bottom of the World					/23
Saving the Children					/23
Queen of the Courts					/20
Exploring Challenger Deep					/23
Life in the Wild					/20
Skiing Down Everest					/20
A Call for Change					/23
Perfect Pitch					/20
Another Way to the Top					/23

Finding Your Score
1. Count the number of correct answers you have for each activity.
2. Write these numbers in the boxes in the chart.
3. Ask your teacher to give you a score (maximum score 5) for **Express Yourself**.
4. Add up the numbers to get a final score.